Ten-Minute
Whole Language Warm-ups

by Murray Suid and Wanda Lincoln

Illustrated by Philip Chalk

This book is for
Anna Suid
and
Jeffrey Goldman

Publisher: Roberta Suid
Editor: Beverly Cory
Design: David Hale
Production: Susan Pinkerton

Other books by the authors: *Book Factory,*
Editing, Greeting Cards, Letter Writing,
More Book Factory, Picture Book Factory,
Report Factory, Research, Sentences,
Stories, Write Through the Year, Writing Hangups.

ISBN 1-878279-38-6

Printed in the United States of America
9 8 7 6 5 4 3 2 1

CONTENTS

INTRODUCTION

This book rests on three simple—but vital—ideas:

1. Skill building does have a place in the whole language classroom. To become competent and creative language artists, children need to know about and practice such varied skills as making effective word choices, editing, researching, creating lively dialogue, and—yes—even getting punctuation and spelling right.

2. Skill-building practices in the whole language classroom must themselves be "whole." The practices provided for students should integrate the language arts. They also should build on the strengths students bring to the activities, so that as students learn the basics, they also use language joyfully.

3. Quick skill practices, if done regularly and tied to the language arts processes, can produce big results. To paraphrase the tortoise, short and steady wins the race.

THE WHOLE LANGUAGE CLASSROOM

In the whole language classroom students are involved in authentic work: reading books, writing for real audiences, talking about ideas, and asking questions. The class is collaborative and student-centered. The focal point is the students' language and their ability to use that language in a variety of situations across the curriculum and in the world outside the classroom. (For a more detailed overview, see "Whole Language at a Glance" in the Resources section.)

POSITIVE PRACTICE

The whole language teacher is a coach who inspires, challenges, observes, and empowers. As with an athletic coach, part of the job is to provide meaningful practices. In the whole language classroom, this means practices that develop key language and thinking skills. The teacher-coach carefully helps students link each practice to the ultimate payoff: playing the real "games" of reading, writing, talking, and listening.

This book offers over seventy such integrated and powerful warm-up activities. These reusable practices are designed to encourage learning through trial and error, to give students choices, to encourage students to take responsibility for creating meaningful work, and to give them access to important ideas. While doing these practices, students have the opportunity to talk and listen to classmates, to draw upon their own background and skills, and to work collaboratively. All this occurs with a simple learning routine: Students try the activities, receive specific and meaningful feedback, and gain skills to use when they do the real work of language: reading, writing, and carrying on conversations. (See "Tips for Effective Practice" on the following page.)

TEN MINUTES AND BEYOND

All of the practices can be done in about ten minutes, though occasionally a bit of preparation may be needed—for example, having the students collect photographs. In most cases, no special materials are required. For some activities, we have provided sample topic lists to help you get started. Items that are used in several practices—for example, fables, homonyms, proverbs—are given in the Resources section.

What if you can find more than ten minutes to invest in the kinds of practices presented here? Every practice activity is accompanied by an open-ended, whole-language project. These in-depth activities are perfect for providing options to those students who have finished their other class work. Or use these extensions to encourage independent learning outside school hours. Many of these projects provide opportunities for creative parental involvement.

ACTIVITY SEQUENCE

The road to literacy is nonlinear. So is this book. You can start anywhere you like: at the beginning, in the middle, or at the end. The skills exercised by a given activity appear in boldface type in the activity overview.

If you want to focus on a specific skill—for example, descriptive writing or vocabulary building—turn to the index. There, you can look up practices according to skills or types of writing.

Whatever path you take into the book, we hope it leads to productive and joyful learning.

Tips for Effective Practice

Introducing a skill

When students are introduced to a new skill or concept, give them many practice opportunities in a short time. Mass practice, at this point, is a productive strategy.

Reinforcing a skill

When students have a growing understanding of a concept or skill, when your goal is to polish or reinforce, distribute the practices over time. Having time elapse between practices at this stage will produce greater results.

Creating effective practices

- Keep practices short. Avoid boredom.

- Vary the formats. In addition to word-based practices, include speaking, listening, drawing, acting, and so on. Consider different learning styles.

- Actively involve students; for example, try to tie activities to the knowledge they bring to the situation.

- Encourage collaboration. Sharing knowledge at this point in the learning process can give the tentative learner a big boost.

- Be clear about the short-term and long-term goals of the activity, and share the goals with the students. This can be as simple as saying something like, "We're practicing using quotation marks today because you'll be using them in your picture-book making project next week."

- Provide immediate feedback. This often involves student self-correction or peer evaluation.

- Do NOT grade practice. Students need to know that practice is a part of learning. At this stage, perfection is not expected. Mistakes are part of the process. Evaluation comes much later, after sufficient practice. (Having students mark a "P" at the top of practice papers helps them differentiate practice from other types of classroom work.)

AS TOLD TO

Movie stars and sports heroes often have their life stories ghostwritten—but why let them have all the glory? Your students can "ghost tell" stories for each other to sharpen **speaking** and **listening** skills.

DIRECTIONS:
1. Have students brainstorm their own lists of topics about their lives. Possibilities include places they have visited, people they know, events they have participated in, and objects that having meaning for them—for example, musical instruments or sports equipment. (Keep the lists in writing folders or journals for use when the practice is repeated.)
2. Tell each student to pick one topic.
3. Divide the class into pairs.
4. For three or five minutes, have one student tell the other about the topic. While the first person talks, the partner takes notes. Explain that it's OK for the listener to ask for clarification or a slower pace.
5. The listener then retells the story.
6. Repeat this activity the following day with the roles reversed.

EXTENSION:
The students turn the notes into complete ghostwritten stories and then bind them into an "As Told To" anthology.

BOOK COVERS

Book covers are usually created after the book is written. But they don't have to be done this way. The task of designing a cover before writing a book can help students identify the **main idea.**

DIRECTIONS:
1. Have each student think up a topic for a children's picture book, for example, a trip to the ballpark or how to make a pizza.
2. Students list several important characters or actions that might be included in the book.
3. Now, they plan the cover of the book. This includes writing a working title and making a rough sketch of the cover art. The idea is to show and tell readers what the book is about,
4. Have students share their preliminary covers in small groups.

EXTENSION:
As an alternative to traditional book reports, students can create new book covers for the books they have read.

CHARACTER NAMES

What do the Big Bad Wolf and the Ugly Duckling have in common? Both characters have wonderfully descriptive names that give clues about the parts they play. Inventing descriptive names provides practice in **fluency** and **character development**.

DIRECTIONS:
1. Have each student choose an animal that could be a character in a story, for example, a camel, a worm, a dinosaur, or a butterfly.
2. Students then brainstorm as many "descriptive" names as they can for their characters. The names, which should suggest something about the animal's personality or behavior, might involve a wording trick such as one of the following:
  • Alliteration—Giggly Goldfish
  • Onomatopoeia—Splashy
  • Rhyme—The Bold Goldfish
  • Name plus descriptive title—Goldy the Great
3. Each student picks a favorite name from the list and briefly tells a partner about the character.

EXTENSION:
Have each student write a story featuring the newly-named character. Students then share their stories in groups.

CHORAL READING

We often think of reading as a solo activity. But the ancient tradition of dramatic group readings gives students a feel for punctuation, the rhythm of words, and the linking of sentences. It also helps sharpen **speaking** and **listening** skills.

DIRECTIONS:
1. Choose a reading with a pattern that's easy to grasp. Poems or stories with refrains are especially appropriate. So are tongue twisters and jump-rope jingles. If the piece is not printed as a choral reading, mark which segments will be *solo*, *small group*, and *whole group*.
2. Explain to students that choral reading is similar to what happens in a band or orchestra. You might even arrange for a demonstration put on by older students.
3. Use hand signals to indicate when students are to join in. Feel free to vary the forms of participation. For example, you might have everyone do the whole reading, or break the class into groups that "talk" to each other.

EXTENSION:
Have students write works expressly designed to be performed by their classmates.

COMICS WITHOUT PICTURES

Translating comic strips into words gives students a chance to practice **descriptive writing**. It also introduces them to the idea of adaptation, converting a work from one form or medium to another.

DIRECTIONS:
1. Provide each student with a different comic strip containing several panels (frames). You might use different installments of the same comic.
2. Have each student turn the comic into a very short prose "story." This will require translating the pictures into words and surrounding the dialogue with quotation marks. The dialogue should be accompanied by dialogue tags such as *she said* or *he laughed*. It's OK to rewrite the dialogue rather than copy the exact words in the dialogue balloons.
3. Each story should have an original title, one that describes or refers to the action presented in the comic.
4. The adapted stories can be read aloud in small groups. After the readings, the writers might show the comic strips they were working from.

EXTENSION:
Students can practice the same process by translating pictures from newspapers, magazines, textbooks, or other publications.

COMING ATTRACTIONS

Careful writers use **transition words**—for example, *however* or *on the other hand*—as verbal signposts to help readers move from one part of a story or essay to the next. Knowing how to understand and use these words is an important reading and writing skill.

DIRECTIONS:
1. Give students a "transition starter"—a short passage that ends with a sentence containing a transition word or phrase. (See following page for models.)
2. Have students, working alone or with a partner, write a sentence or paragraph that logically would follow the given text.
3. Share the writing in small groups.

EXTENSION:
Make a bulletin board of transition sentences that students find in their ongoing reading.

Transition Starters

I always thought that spiders were yucky. Whenever I saw one spinning a web, I'd run away as fast as I could. However,...

The monster was fast asleep. I had to wake him quickly, but I could think of only three ways to do it. First, I could shout. Second, I could...

The two dogs stopped barking and began to wag their tails. Then, they...

The once-beautiful model airplane lay crumpled in a mud puddle. Its left wing was broken in three places. Its right wing was nowhere to be seen. Who could believe that just five minutes earlier...

The bully stood right in front of me but was looking the other way. I could try to run away. Or...

On the one hand, I felt that I just had to have that new coat. It looked so warm and soft. The colors were perfect for me. On the other hand...

More Transition Words and Phrases
At the same time...
Earlier...
Even better (worse)...
Fortunately...
Later...
Meanwhile...
Moreover...
Nevertheless...
Still...
Unfortunately...
While this was happening...

DESCRIPTIVE DETAIL

Writing that merely tells a fact can be boring, for example: "The wind blew hard." That's why successful writers usually use **detail-rich sentences** that show as well as tell.

DIRECTIONS:

1. On the board present a "telling" sentence, for example, "The bath water was hot." (See the next page for additional telling sentences.)

2. Challenge students to write as many "showing" sentences as they can that get across the idea in the telling sentence. For example:

- Steam rose from the bath water.
- Jerry stuck his foot into the bath and screamed, "I burned my toe!"
- The thermometer in the tub read 120 degrees F.

3. Have students share their sentences in small groups.

EXTENSION:

Each student writes an original "show-not-tell" paragraph without stating the key fact. Other students then try to name the fact. For example:

The wood on the porch glistened. I stepped out the door and slid down the stairs. (Key fact: *The porch was icy.*)

Ten-foot-long icicles hung from the roof.

IT WAS COLD!

Sentences to Rewrite

The food looks good.

That was a scary movie.

The radio was too loud.

The car went down the street very quickly.

The nearby lightning made a bright flash.

I don't have very much money.

That dog looks fierce.

There is a deep hole in the street.

The spelling test was difficult.

Their garage is messy.

The cloth in that shirt feels rough.

The directions to your house are complicated.

She plays the piano beautifully.

That basketball player is very tall.

This box weighs a lot.

The orange tastes sour.

The potato chip bag was hard to open.

The old man's beard was very long.

The diamond was worth a great deal of money.

The eagle flew gracefully.

Our car is old.

Her friend is happy.

We waited in a long line.

The water in the swimming pool is very cold.

The lock on my bicycle is very strong.

That hat is really expensive.

My cousin has a good memory.

That garbage smells awful.

The sidewalk is hot.

DESCRIPTIVE DIALOGUE

Story writers often have their characters talk about what they see. This **descriptive writing** technique can add interest and realism.

DIRECTIONS:

1. Choose something to describe. It could be a real object in the room, for example, a half-eaten apple; or it could be a scene in a photograph.

2. Students make up two or three characters and write dialogue in which they talk about the thing. For example:

> "What's that on the desk?" asked Francis.
> "It's an apple," said Myrna, "a Pippin."
> "Someone's been eating it," added Ralph.

3. Share the descriptive passages orally.

EXTENSION:

Have students look for and share descriptive dialogue that they find in stories and novels.

DIALOGUE TAGS

The *way* a character talks can be as important as *what* the character says. That's why writers are careful about how they tag **dialogue**.

DIRECTIONS:
1. With the students, list a variety of dialogue tags on the board. Examples include *whispered*, *laughed*, *replied*, *shouted*, and *said with a quivering voice*. (See following page for more examples.)
2. Give the students a sentence, for example:

"Come with me."

3. Have students repeat the sentence using various tags. They should, of course, interpret the dialogue according to the tag:

"Come with me," he whispered.
"Come with me," she commanded.
"Come with me," her cousin mumbled.

EXTENSION:
Have students create a bulletin board with examples of tagged dialogue found in the literature books they are reading.

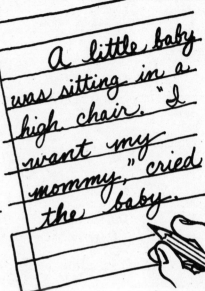

17

Dialogue Tags

acknowledged	muttered
admitted	nagged
agreed	pleaded
answered	promised
argued	questioned
asked	remembered
barked	replied
begged	requested
bellowed	retorted
blustered	roared
bragged	sang
complained	screamed
confessed	screeched
cried	shouted
demanded	sighed
denied	snarled
giggled	sobbed
hinted	threatened
hissed	wailed
howled	warned
inquired	whimpered
interrupted	whined
laughed	whispered
lied	wondered
mumbled	yelled

DO YOU SEE WHAT I MEAN?

Descriptive writing means sending a picture from the writer's mind to the reader's mind. By describing simple diagrams, students can quickly evaluate their skills at creating clear messages. The task also gives practice in attentive **listening**.

DIRECTIONS:

1. Have each student make a simple diagram on a piece of paper. The diagrams should not be shown to anyone.
2. Students next write descriptions of their diagrams. For example:

> In the center of a triangle with three equal sides is a large X. The X is not touching any part of the triangle. Around the entire triangle, but also not touching it, is a circle.

3. Divide the class into pairs.
4. Taking turns, students read aloud their description while their partners draw what they see in their minds. If a drawer needs clarification, the writer should feel free to modify the description.
5. When finished, partners should compare their drawings and discuss reasons for any discrepancies.

EXTENSION:

Have one student read a description of a diagram while the whole class draws it. Have students compare their drawings.

EAR FOR PUNCTUATION

Listening to a sentence read aloud can often help a writer figure out the **punctuation** that is needed.

DIRECTIONS:
1. Ahead of time, find a passage in a book that contains several punctuation marks familiar to the students. Retype the passage leaving out all punctuation marks.
2. Give a copy of the unpunctuated passage to each student.
3. Read the passage aloud to the class, allowing your voice to indicate where punctuation marks are needed. Encourage students to insert the needed punctuation marks.
4. Working in small groups, students then compare their punctuation decisions.
5. Show or tell the students what marks were in the original so that they can compare their punctuation with that done by a professional writer.

EXTENSION:
Make a bulletin board of punctuation marks that students find in their reading.

EXACTLY WRITE

Look up in the sky. Is it an animal...a bird...or an... eagle? Working with word sequences—from general to specific—gives students practice in the art of effective **word choice**.

DIRECTIONS:
1. Use concentric circles (circles within circles) to show the sequence of a set of words from general to specific.
2. On the board list three to five related words—for example, toy, checkers, board game, thing—and have students arrange the words from general to specific.
3. Finally, give students a single word and ask them to suggest other words that might be more specific. (See following page for some starter words.) Note that a given word may lead to different sequences, for example:

   liquid, water, cold water, ice water
   liquid, soup, chicken soup, chicken noodle soup
   liquid, gasoline, unleaded gas

EXTENSION:
Give students "mock manuscripts" that include very general words. Have them replace these words with more precise terms.

Word Sequence Starters

activity

animal

bird

book

city

clothing

color

container

dream

entertainer

food

furniture

game

hobby

insect

letter (of the alphabet)

liquid

money

movie

music

musical instrument

number

pain

picture

place

plant

relative

store

tool

toy

weapon

weather

worker

EYE SEARCH RIDDLES

Research doesn't mean finding facts only in books. Reporters, scientists, and writers use all their powers of **observation** to learn about the world. The following activity uses eyewitness data in a guessing game.

DIRECTIONS:
1. Divide the class into groups of two or three.
2. Give each group an object to study, for example, a toothbrush. Each group should keep their object hidden from the other groups.
3. Have the students record all the facts they can about the object based on firsthand observation. These notes may use words or diagrams or both.
4. Have each group share their facts orally with another group, whose members then try to guess what the object is.

EXTENSION:
Have students write stories that use eyewitness details. For example, a story might include a scene in the classroom, on the playground, or even in the principal's office.

FACT SCAVENGER HUNT

The key to successful **research** is being aware of the wide variety of reference books available in the library.

Note: Do this activity in the library or simply bring the reference books to your room.

DIRECTIONS:
1. Gather a variety of reference books, for example, almanacs, atlases, biographical dictionaries, encyclopedias, and quotation books.
2. Divide the class into small groups.
3. Give each group a different reference book and ask them to locate at least three interesting facts in it.
4. Share the facts with the whole class.

EXTENSION:
Have teams of students carry out library scavenger hunts using lists like the one on the following page.

Scavenger Hunt List

Answer each question and name the book where you found the information.

1. Who invented the parachute?

2. What does a gnu eat?

3. Name five kinds of clocks.

4. What star is closest to the earth?

5. How many people live in Edmonton?

6. Give an example of a hardwood tree.

7. What is an amoeba?

8. How many calories are there in an egg?

9. What is Edmund Hillary famous for?

10. List four craters on the moon.

11. What is the name of the first atomic submarine?

12. Can a worm see?

FIGURATIVELY SPEAKING

Because TV is so literal, it doesn't provide practice in decoding or enjoying **metaphorical messages**. But rather than cry over spilled milk, try this proverb-explaining activity that gives students at least a half of loaf of wisdom.

DIRECTIONS:
1. Write a proverb on the board, for example: "No use crying over spilled milk." (See Resources for more proverbs.)
2. Lead a brief discussion to make sure that the students understand the literal meaning of the statement.
3. Ask students, working alone or with partners, to find examples from life that illustrate the truth of the saying. For example:

> That's like you had a chance to go on a trip but didn't go, and then later you complain that you should have gone. But it's too late to do anything about it.

4. Share the stories.

EXTENSION:
Create a class book of personal experiences or made-up stories, each of which demonstrates the truth of a given proverb. In each case, the proverb can be used as the title of the story.

FISHING FOR THE RIGHT WORD

Like most good writers, Robert Louis Stevenson cared about **word choice**. He once crossed out a word and tried another. On the eighth try, he found the word he wanted—the first he had tried.

DIRECTIONS:

1. Write a sentence on the board, leaving out a noun, adjective, verb, or adverb:

I watched the _____ insect.

If students have studied parts of speech, label the slot to reinforce previous learning:

I watched the _____ insect.
                    adjective

2. Ask each student or student team to list as many words as they can that would make sense in the blank(s). In the sentence above, possible adjectives are *big, busy, interesting,* and *quick-moving.*

3. For a greater challenge, leave out a phrase:

We found the missing key _____ _____ _____.

Possible phrases are "on the table" or "near my boot."

EXTENSION:

Have students create participation stories in which readers fill in descriptive words or phrases.

27

FOLLOW THE READER

You can teach students about feedback by having them read aloud messages that require careful **listening**.

DIRECTIONS:
1. Choose (or have students write) short pieces that invite the reader or listener to do something. A simple example is "Simon Says." (See the following pages for other models.)
2. Read—or have a student read—the words as the rest of the class "performs."

EXTENSION:
Have students create their own performance works which classmates can then bring to life.

Follow the Reader Materials

These items may also serve as models for teacher-written or student-written audience-participation readings.

Hand Movements

Listeners use hand gestures to illustrate the main actions in a nursery rhyme or poem.

Jack and Jill
Went up the hill (hands going up)
To fetch
A pail of water. (hands cupped)
Jack fell down
And broke his crown. (hands clasped to head)
And Jill came
Tumbling after. (hands tumbling over each other)

Twinkle, twinkle (fingers fluttering)
Little star
How I wonder (finger on chin)
What you are.
Up above (finger points upward)
The world so high
Like a diamond
In the sky.

A horse galloped up a mountain.
   (fingers make galloping motion upward)
From the top its rider could see
   (shield eyes as if looking)
the ocean's waves.
   (make waving motion)
In the ocean a whale swam and then dived under the water.
   (hand as whale dives downward)
An octopus tried to grab the whale.
   (one hand, fingers akimbo, grabs the "whale" hand)
But the whale twisted its body and escaped.
   ("whale" twists and turns)

Clap for a Word

The reader invites the listeners to signal when a certain kind of word is heard. It might be a word that starts or ends with a given letter, or a word that rhymes with a given word.

Listen carefully. Every time I say a word that begins with "r" I want you to clap your hands once. Ready? (If no one claps, repeat "Ready.")

The other day I went to a rodeo with my family. There, we saw cowboys and cowgirls riding horses round and round. Their horses were bright red. Not really. They were actually brown.

When we got hungry, we ate hot dogs and drank root beer.

Back at our seats, we watched the performers twirl their ropes. After a few hours, it was time to go home. On the way, we saw lightning and rain. I climbed into bed happy but really tired.

Sound Effects

Listeners (using their mouths, fingers, or simple objects) make noises that fit into the story.

I was in my room when I heard the teakettle whistle (gesture to the audience to make the sound). I ran (sound) to turn it off. I poured the water into a cup (sound). Then I opened a kitchen cabinet door, found a hard cookie, and began to eat it (sound).

Direction Pointing

Listeners indicate where an action will take place: up/down, left/right, in/out, over/under, etc.

One day I was out walking and saw a cloud. I looked at my baby sister who was crawling on the ground... etc.

Stand-up Stories

Listeners stand up whenever there is an upward action. Then they sit right down until the next "stand-up" action.

One day I woke up and got out of bed. I looked out the window and saw a strange vine.

FOR EXAMPLE

The following **brainstorming** activity gives students
practice in finding examples, a secret ingredient in lively
and original writing.

DIRECTIONS:
1. Divide the class into small groups.
2. Give the students a topic such as "yellow things." (See
following page for sample topics.)
3. Have students, working alone or in small groups, list
as many examples as they can that fit the topic or
category.
4. Share the lists orally or post them.

EXTENSION:
Have students write example-rich picture books. A
delightful model is Judith Viorst's *Alexander and the
Terrible, Horrible, No Good, Very Bad Day.*

Brainstorming Topics

Activities that can be done with an animal

Activities that must be done outdoors

Activities that require practice

Animal characters

Animals that live with people

Animals with tails

Games played outdoors

Letters of the alphabet formed with straight lines

Places that are usually dark

Places where it's OK to make noise

Reasons for not watching television

Reasons for sharing things

Reasons for smiling at people

Sports in which time is important

Surprises that are pleasant

Surprises that are unpleasant

Things found in a school room

Things that break easily

Things that change shape when used

Things that move in a circle

Things that fall

Things that hang

Things that make noise when in use

Things that make no noise when in use

Uses of the telephone

Uses of walls

Ways to show friendship

Words a dog might use if a dog could talk

Words that start and end with the same letter

Words used when leaving someone

GIVE ME A BREAK

Effective **sentence writing** requires awareness of where sentences begin and end.

DIRECTIONS:
1. Find a paragraph with at least three sentences. The paragraph can be fiction or nonfiction. A good source is your social studies or science text.
2. Write the passage on the board as if it were a single sentence. That is, do not capitalize the first word of any sentence except the first one, and omit end punctuation except after the last sentence.
3. Have students break the passage into sentences. They can do this individually on paper, or, if working in small groups, by discussing the breaks orally.
4. After students understand the activity, they can create "give me a break" worksheets for each other.

EXTENSION:
If you have students who don't pay enough attention to inserting spaces between words, do the same activity using a single sentence with spaces omitted between the words.

GOOD STARTS

An important part of any piece of writing is the first sentence or paragraph, which is called the *lead*. The lead has two jobs: to capture the reader's attention and to introduce the subject. Practicing writing leads is a sure-fire way to strengthen the skill of **drafting**.

DIRECTIONS:
1. Choose a topic that students could write about without doing library research, for example, "Having a bad dream" or "Doing homework."
2. Have students write three different leads for an article or story about the chosen topic. Each lead can be the same type of lead, such as a quotation. Or each might be a different type, for example, a quotation, an action, an opinion. (Some different types of leads are listed on the following page.)
3. Students can share their leads in small groups.

EXTENSION:
Find an example of each type of lead in newspapers, magazines, books, or other kinds of writing. Make a bulletin board of the different types.

Common Types of Leads

Action lead: Something happens.

The ball sailed over the fence and crashed into the window of a second-floor apartment.

Character lead: Someone is pictured.

The old man sat on a bench reading a newspaper. He was all dressed up in a suit and tie. The only odd thing about him was the baseball cap that sat backward on his head.

Fact lead: A piece of information is given.

The largest crossword puzzle ever published had more than 5000 clues across and a similar number down.

Opinion lead: A belief is stated.

Cats are a thousand times nicer than dogs.

Question lead: A question or a series of questions is asked.

Can dreams predict the future?

Quotation lead: Words are taken from another context.

"Always chew your food slowly," my mother used to tell me.

Single word lead: An important word is set off by itself, and then followed by explanatory sentences.

Mud. Mud was everywhere. It was on the rug. It was on the walls. It was on the furniture. I had never seen so much mud in my life.

HEADLINE HELPER

Recognizing the **main idea** in a speech or piece of writing is a key **reading comprehension** skill.

DIRECTIONS:
1. Read aloud—or have a student read aloud—a short news story with the headline removed.
2. Encourage note-taking during the reading. This could involve listing key words or phrases.
3. Have students write two or three headlines that fit the story and relate to the main idea. Each should then circle a favorite.
4. In small groups, have students share and discuss their headlines.

EXTENSION:
Make a bulletin board of clever newspaper headlines collected by students. Include examples from all sections of the newspaper. (Sports headlines are often especially witty.) Follow up with a bulletin board of student-written headlines.

HOMONYM SENTENCES

The most common **spelling** errors involve sound-alike words. Writing sentences that correctly use homonyms can help solve the problem.

DIRECTIONS:
1. Write a pair or trio of homonyms on the board. For example:
   right—write
   pair—pear—pare
You'll find a list of homonyms in the Resources section.
2. Include a definition of each word or make sure dictionaries are handy.
3. Have students use each pair in a single sentence.
   Is this the *right* way to *write* a letter?
   Please *pare* me a *pair* of *pears*.
Illustrating these sentences with cartoon characters can add fun.

EXTENSION:
Turn the homonym sentences into homonym riddles by blanking out the sound-alike words and by adding contextual clues:

   Please _____ me a _____ of those juicy Bartlett
   _____, which I will then bake in a pie for dessert.

Collect a number of the riddles into a riddle book.

HOW TO DO IT

Teaching a how-to-do-it lesson gives practice in clear thinking and logical **sequencing**.

DIRECTIONS:
1. Tell students to list several simple activities that they actually know how to do. For the sake of originality, avoid "making a peanut butter sandwich." (See examples on following page.)
2. Have each student or small group pick an activity and describe how to do it in half a dozen or so steps.
3. Share the directions in small groups.

EXTENSION:
Have advanced students write well-researched "direction reports" on more difficult subjects such as landing a 747 or milking a cow. This research might involve interviewing experts.

OK, THE FIRST STEP IS...

How-to-do-it Topics

Everyday Tasks

Alphabetize words

Brush teeth

Build a sand castle

Call someone on the phone

Change a light bulb

Cross a street safely

Eat with chopsticks

Find a nonfiction book

Finger paint

Give a dog a bath

Jump rope

Make popcorn

Play hopscotch

Play tic-tac-toe

Report an emergency to 911

Ride a bicycle

Set the table

Take a bath

Tell time

Thread a needle

Tie a bow

Vacuum a rug

Watch a scary movie

Welcome a new student

Whistle

Write a thank-you note

Expert Tasks

Act in a Hollywood movie

Argue a case before a jury

Drive a race car

Fly a jet plane

Forecast the weather

Gather honey from a hive

Knit a sweater

Make a stained-glass picture

Parachute from an airplane

Play the harp, violin, etc.

Pole vault

Ride a bucking bronco

Run a restaurant

Sail a boat

Set a broken bone

Take out an appendix

Throw a curve ball

Walk on a tightrope

Wash windows of a skyscraper

Write a computer program

I AM THE UGLY DUCKLING

Character development is a key issue in fiction. One way to help students grasp this concept is to bring characters to life.

DIRECTIONS:
1. After hearing or reading a story, choose a character and ask students to brainstorm adjectives that describe that character. For example, the Ugly Duckling might be called *lonely*, *different*, and *unhappy*. Peter Rabbit might be labeled *sneaky*, *naughty*, and *foolish*.
2. Divide the class into groups of four or five. One student in each group should pretend to be the character and answer questions asked by the other members of the group. The adjectives will help the role-playing student stay in character.

EXTENSION:
Have students give role-play book reports in which they talk to the class from the point of view of one of the characters in their reading.

IMAGINE THIS

Paintings by Norman Rockwell, Grandma Moses, and other artists can serve as stimuli for strengthening **descriptive writing** and **reading comprehension** skills. The following activity also involves **listening**.

DIRECTIONS:
1. Find a print of a visually striking painting such as Vincent van Gogh's "Starry, Starry Night." Do not show the picture to the class. Another option is to use an illustration from an unfamiliar picture book. (See following page for painters and illustrators you might use.)
2. Have the students close their eyes while you describe the picture. Or, better, have a student do the describing.
3. When the description is completed, tell students to open their eyes and compare what they imagined with the real picture. They can add details that the describer overlooked.

EXTENSION:
Read a descriptive passage from a story. Have the students draw what they "see" in their minds while listening.

Pictures to Describe

Art supply and frame shops sell inexpensive prints by well-known artists. Look for the following:

Mary Cassatt
Leonardo da Vinci
Edgar Degas
Paul Gauguin
René Magritte
Edouard Manet
Michelangelo
Claude Monet
Grandma Moses
Pablo Picasso
Pierre Auguste Renoir
Norman Rockwell
Henri Rousseau
Georges Seurat
Gilbert Charles Stuart
Vincent van Gogh

Children's libraries and bookstores are filled with imagination-stirring art by illustrators such as:

Aliki
Lynne Cherry
Tom Feelings
Tomie de Paola
Clement Hurd
Trina Schart Hyman
Susan Jeffers
Steven Kellogg
Arnold Lobel
Mercer Mayer
Peter Parnall
Maurice Sendak
Margot Zemach

IN OTHER WORDS

The skill of **paraphrasing** can be developed through
repeated short exercises. In other words, little by little
wins the race.

DIRECTIONS:

1. Write a proverb or other memorable sentence on the
board. You'll find a list of proverbs in the Resource
section of this book.

2. Ask students, working alone or in small groups, to
carefully read the statement and then replace all the
important words, while trying to keep the meaning.
You might use underlining to indicate the important
words. In some cases, two or three words may be needed
to replace one word in the original. For example:

A bird in the hand is worth two in the bush.

One robin or other winged animal that you can hold
equals double that number who are making a tree-like
plant their home.

EXTENSION:

Have students paraphrase haiku, limericks, dialogue in
comic strips, or other short pieces.

INTERVIEWED OBJECTS

One skill is shared by reporters, inventors, teachers, and most other smart people: asking good **questions**. Students can sharpen this skill by interviewing inanimate objects. At the same time, they'll practice **personification**.

ASK WHATEVER YOU WANT!

DIRECTIONS:

1. Have the class brainstorm a list of everyday objects, such as a pencil, a TV, or a bicycle.
2. Each student chooses one object and then lists two to five questions that the object might answer if it were able to think and talk.
3. Students then write short "Question and Answer" interviews of their objects. For example:

A Pencil Tells All

Question: What do you enjoy most in life?
Answer: Helping people write stories and draw pictures.
Question: Do you ever hate being a pencil?
Answer: Sure. When I have to get sharpened.

During this step it's perfectly OK for students to think up and ask questions that were not on their original lists.
4. Share interviews through oral reading or by posting them on a bulletin board.

EXTENSION:

Do the same activity, but base the questions and answers on library research. This way students might interview plants, states, provinces, countries, unusual animals, and inventions.

I'VE GOT A FEW QUESTIONS FOR YOU!

IS THAT A FACT?

Knowing the difference between facts and opinions is essential for **reading comprehension** and **research**.

DIRECTIONS:
1. On the board, list several fact statements about the classroom and several opinion statements.

> Facts:
> The lights are on.
> There are flowers on the teacher's desk.
> Opinions:
> The aquarium is the most interesting thing in the room.
> The clock is beautiful.

Explain that a fact is a statement whose truth can be checked by observation—using one or more senses. There's no way to show that "Chocolate ice cream tastes best." But a person can weigh two bricks to see which is heavier.
2. Choose another topic and have students list at least three fact statements and three opinion statements. (See following page for topics.)
3. Share the facts and opinions.

EXTENSION:
Have students identify fact statements in their reading. This activity can even take the form of a book review, for example, "Five Fact Statements in *Make Way for Ducklings*."

Water freezes faster than oil.

Water tastes better than soda.

Fact or Opinion Topics

character in a story

city or town where the school is located

computers

desk or any other piece of furniture in the room

dictionary

doing the dishes

eye or other part of the head

field trip recently taken

fire drills

flag in room

Halloween or any other holiday

June or any other month

last night's dinner

Main Street or any other street in town

map or globe in room

moon or other heavenly bodies

peanut butter or any other food

rain

roller blades

rose or any other plant

Saturday or any other day of the week

school subject

school's playground

sport the students play

taking a bath

telephone

textbook

TV—in general

TV—particular program

view out the classroom window

JOURNAL WRITING

Many successful writers, actors, and language lovers are good at **getting ideas** because they take time to capture their experiences in a journal or diary.

DIRECTIONS:
1. Introduce the activity by reading a few passages from a published journal, for example, *Harriet the Spy*.
2. In the tradition of Sustained Silent Reading, budget ten minutes regularly—daily, if possible—for students to set down their thoughts, concerns, questions, or impressions.
3. Encourage students to add drawings, clippings from magazines, and objects such as tickets or photographs.

EXTENSION:
Have students use their journals when they are searching for writing topics.

Note: To ensure privacy, you might wish to have students store their journals in a locked cabinet or desk drawer.

KEY IDEA SEARCH

Learning to spot the **main idea** of a paragraph is a crucial **reading comprehension** skill. It also paves the way to writing well-focused summaries.

DIRECTIONS:
1. Give students a short article or excerpt from a longer work. The piece should have at least two paragraphs.
2. Have students, working alone or with partners, read each paragraph and state the main idea in a short sentence—five or fewer words. The more concise the summary, the more thinking is involved.
3. Have students share the summaries with the entire class.

EXTENSION:
Have students write single-sentence summaries of paragraphs from math, science, social studies and other textbooks or study materials. They could also summarize reports written by classmates.

LANGUAGE CATCH

Taking dictation sharpens **listening** skills while providing valuable practice with **punctuation**.

DIRECTIONS:
1. Ahead of time—perhaps for homework—have each student find and rehearse a joke, a poem, or any short piece of writing. Limit the presentation time to about one minute.
2. Divide the class into pairs. The students will then read their selections aloud to their partners (scribes) who will try to capture the words exactly. Readers should pause from time to time to allow the scribes to catch up or ask for a phrase to be repeated.
3. When the readings are finished, give the scribes time to compare their versions with the originals and make required corrections in punctuation and spelling.

EXTENSION:
After students become proficient at taking dictation, you might have them act as scribes for younger children.

LIVING PUPPETS

Writing plays is one of the best activities for learning that language arts is about communication. The following playwriting activity provides practice in giving and **following directions**.

DIRECTIONS:
1. Have the students write pantomime playlets to be performed by a classmate. For example:

> You are a seed. It is warm out and you begin to grow. You become a plant. You grow taller and taller. Now as a wind comes you sway to the left and to the right.

Each "script" should contain three or four actions that could easily be performed in the classroom without props. The scripts can focus entirely on gestures or they might include a few spoken words.
2. Each student reads the script to a partner. The partner listens, asks for clarification if needed, and then acts out the motions. The "playwright" gives the actor feedback and suggestions.

EXTENSION:
Students can write longer plays to be performed for the entire class.

LOOK WHAT'S TALKING

Personifying objects or animals can add interest to stories, reports, and other kinds of writing.

Before doing this practice, create a personification bulletin board. Students can find examples in their reading and in TV commercials, which often feature talking tunas and other "smart" products.

DIRECTIONS:

1. Ask each student to pick a thing that's not alive and that they know some facts about, for example, a bicycle or a cloud. (See next page for other objects to personify.)
2. After discussing the object with a partner, each student writes a short passage in which the chosen object talks about itself. For example:

> I'm a ten-speed bicycle. You can call me Speedy. When I'm standing still, I'm not very steady on my feet—I mean wheels. But once I get going, my balance is super.

3. Have students share their personifications in small groups.

EXTENSION:

Have students write autobiographical or biographical "thing-ographies" in which the important things in a person's life "talk" about that person. For example, a "thing-ography" about a baseball player might feature comments about the person by a baseball glove, a bat, and a ball.

TO YOU, I'M JUST A FIRE PLUG, BUT I SEE MYSELF AS A LIFE SAVER.

Objects to Personify

airplane

animal (fly, worm, etc.)

bed

bicycle

book

car

chair

clock

closet

clothing (shirt, shoes, etc.)

computer

dictionary

eraser

eyeglasses

floor

flower

frying pan

food (carrots, pastry, etc.)

fork

lightning

garbage can

magnifying glass

mirror

money

moon

newspaper

ocean

pencil

penny

radio

rain cloud

refrigerator

report card

roller coaster

rug

school

sink

soap

sports equipment (baseball, bat, etc.)

street

sun

swing

telephone

television

thunder

toothbrush

tree

vacuum cleaner

washing machine

MAKE EVERY WORD COUNT

It sometimes makes sense to specify the number of words in an assignment. This kind of limitation can help develop **editing** skills.

DIRECTIONS:
1. Choose a topic students can easily write about, for example, hobbies, friends, sports, or favorite books.
2. Have students describe or write about the subject using a set number of words, for example, 25.
3. Students share their efforts in small groups.

EXTENSION:
Sometimes, give precise word limits to book reviews, research papers, or other traditional assignments. Or try time limits on oral presentations, for example, a two-minute math talk explaining denominators.

MARRIED WORDS

Learning about the origins of words (etymology) lays the foundation for **vocabulary building**. Studying compound words is an easy and logical place to begin.

DIRECTIONS:
1. Be sure students know what a compound word is. One way to get across the concept is to divide a few examples on the board.
2. Now, write another compound word on the board, for example: *earring*. (See next page for other compound words.)
3. Have students, working alone or with partners, break the word into its two "base" words: *ear + ring*.
4. Students then brainstorm as many words and phases as they can that relate to each base word. For example:

   ear: earplug, ear of corn, in one ear and out the other
   ring: ring around the collar, wedding ring, napkin
       ring, ring finger

5. Share the lists on the board.

EXTENSION:
Make a bulletin board that gives the interesting stories of word histories.

Compound Words

airplane	girlfriend
anybody	heartache
backbend	highchair
bagpipe	lighthouse
baseball	milkshake
boyfriend	notebook
breakfast	potholder
campfire	railroad
chalkboard	rainbow
cookout	runway
cowboy	sandbox
doorbell	sidewalk
doughnut	skyscraper
dragonfly	thumbtack
earring	toothache
eyeglasses	undertow
farmhouse	waterfall
firefighter	workbook
fishpond	

MEMORY WRITING

A novelist once said that "Nothing is wasted in a writer's life." All memories have value. Bringing them to mind is an essential part of **getting ideas**.

DIRECTIONS:
1. Give students a key word or phrase, for example, "a good time with a friend" or "a scary moment."
2. Ask students to spend several minutes recalling ideas and mental pictures relating to the topic.
3. When they feel ready, students write about the topic for five minutes. The goal is not to produce a polished essay, but simply to capture remembered details.
4. Invite students to share their memories in small groups but, because some recollections may be very personal, don't require sharing.

EXTENSION:
Have students, working in pairs, create a group memory of a shared experience, for example, what happened "when the lights went out during the big storm."

Memorable Moments

eating a strange food

fight with a friend

first ride in an airplane

first ride on a two-wheeler

getting a pet

getting lost

giving someone a perfect present

going through a storm

having an accident

having the hiccups

laughing about something

learning to operate a piece of equipment, for example, a
   remote-control toy

losing something

making a good play in some sport

making something, for example, a clay pot or a paper
   airplane

meeting a famous person

performing in front of an audience

saying goodbye to a friend who moved away

seeing a favorite film

solving a tricky problem

starting a hobby

surprise party

teaching someone how to do something

visit to a dentist

visiting a different city

winning an award at school, in scouting, etc.

MOCK EDITING

Editing and **revising** are key steps in the writing process. An efficient way to improve these skills is through practice on mock manuscripts with errors inserted by the teacher.

DIRECTIONS:

1. Prepare a short mock manuscript of error-filled writing. Choose problems found in the students' writing or previously studied in class, for example, confusing homonyms (there/their). The manuscript may take the form of a story, a letter, a report, a poem, or other assignment. (See next page for a sample.)

2. Hand out the mock manuscript. Encourage students to read it over before beginning to make corrections.

3. Working alone or with a partner, students correct errors in content and mechanics. (See page after next for edited sample.)

4. Follow up with a whole-class discussion about the changes. Encourage students to give reasons for each modification. Students who overlooked needed changes should make them during the discussion.

EXTENSION:

Instead of correcting the mock manuscript, student editors can mark errors in the margin, using standard proofreaders' marks. This practice will help prepare students for peer editing. (Standard proofreaders' marks can be found in many dictionaries.)

58

Sample "Mock" Manuscript

1   **Review**

2   Would you like to build a flying saucer and have

3   adventures all around the world Would you like to

4   to a trip to the moon. If you answered yes then your

5   going to enjoy reading Sue Howards new science fiction

6   the Great Flying Saucer Hoax. The book tell the story

7   of 2 teenage boys, Rob and Peter. Rob loves machines.

8   Peter loves adventure. One day, Peter learns that Rob

9   has invent an anti-gravity machine. He tells Rob that

10   they should build a flying saucer and then visit

11   Europe, Asia, and other placces. Rob agrees. After a

12   few months, they begin to fly different places. While

13   have fun, they accidentally scare people in many

14   and cause all sorts of problems to have. By the end of

15   the story, the two friends learn that its important to

16   to think about other people.

Edited "Mock" Manuscript

1   **Review**

2   ¶ Would you like to build a flying saucer and have

3   adventures ~~all~~ around the world! Would you like to

4   ~~to~~ *take* a trip to the moon? If you answered "yes," then ~~your~~ *you're*

5   going to enjoy reading Sue Howard's new science fiction *novel,*

6   ~~the~~ *¶* the <u>Great</u> <u>Flying</u> <u>Saucer</u> <u>Hoax</u>. The book tells the story

7   of ~~2~~ *two* teenage boys, Rob and Peter. Rob loves machines.

8   Peter loves adventure. One day, Peter learns that Rob

9   has ~~invent~~ *invented* an anti-gravity machine. He tells Rob that

10   they should build a flying saucer and then visit

11   Europe, Asia, and other places. Rob agrees. After a

12   few months, they begin to fly *to* different places. While

13   ~~have~~ *having* fun, they accidentally scare people in many *lands*

14   and cause all sorts of problems to ~~have~~. *happen* ¶ By the end of

15   the story, the two friends learn that ~~its~~ *it's* important to

16   ~~to~~ think about other people.

MY WORDS DIARY

An early step in creating a poem, a story, an article, or almost any kind of writing is **brainstorming**. In this important **prewriting** activity, the writer lists words and phrases that help uncover important ideas and examples.

DIRECTIONS:
1. Have students list several words or phrases that come to mind when they think about what they did during the past 24 hours.
2. With a partner, students can talk about one or more of the listed words for a few minutes.

EXTENSION:
Encourage students to use this "key word" strategy when working on all sorts of assignments. For example, before writing a book report, students might list three or four key words that the book makes them think about.

NOTE CARD OUTLINE

Screenwriters plan their movies by describing each scene on a note card using only a few words. This hands-on **outlining** technique makes it easier to rearrange the parts than if the outline took the traditional form of a list.

DIRECTIONS:
1. Break the class into small groups. Give each group about ten note cards.
2. Have each group choose a familiar story such as a fable or a fairy tale. (See Resources for a collection of fables.)
3. The groups then describe each important scene in the story on a separate card. Imposing a five-word limit per card forces students to zero in on key ideas. (Students who finish early might add cards covering possible new scenes for the old story. Or they could try to reorder the events.)

EXTENSION:
Have students create cards before writing their own stories. They can "test" their stories with partners by orally describing the action as they go through the cards.

"OOPS, I MADE A MISTOOK"

Everyone makes misteaks—that is, mistakes. The secret is learning to learn from those errors. Studies show that **analyzing mistakes** and logging them in a notebook leads to improvement in spelling, punctuation, word choice, and sentence structure.

DIRECTIONS:
1. Have students keep an error section in their notebooks. They should set up a separate page for each important type of mistake, for example, capitalization, punctuation, spelling, and word choice.
2. Whenever the teacher or a peer editor spots an error in the student's work, the student writes the corrected word or sentence on the appropriate error page.
When possible, students should write comments to help themselves avoid repeating mistakes. For example, "*High school* is two words, just like *elementary school.*"

EXTENSION:
Use the same error-noting technique in math and other curriculum areas.

PICTURES IN THE NEWS

A picture can help a speaker zero in on a story's **main idea**. Working with visuals from a newspaper can also build interest in current events.

Ahead of time, have each student bring to class a newspaper or magazine article illustrated by an interesting photograph or drawing. Ask students to read the accompanying text or have an older person read it to them.

DIRECTIONS:

1. On the board list the classic "five w's" to help students think about their pictures: Who? What? Where? Why? and When?
2. Divide the class into small groups.
3. Have students give brief talks about their pictures. Their mini-presentations should answer at least two of the five questions.

EXTENSION:

Two or more students can use photos to create stick-puppet characters who carry on a dialogue dealing with an important current events topic.

I'm a new Star-burst rocket launched for the first time last night from Cape Canaveral. My job is to...

POINT-OF-VIEW SURPRISES

Varying **point of view** is a technique that can add creativity to **descriptive writing** assignments.

DIRECTIONS:
1. Choose a familiar subject to describe, for example, the classroom.
2. Ask students to pick an unusual point of view from which that subject might be observed, for example, looking down on the classroom from the ceiling.
3. Students use their imaginations to picture the subject—in words or through a drawing—from the given point of view.

EXTENSION:
Get an aerial photograph of your town or neighborhood and have students describe what they see. Such photographs are available from regional or county planning departments. Aerial photo companies are another source. (See "Photographers-Aerial" in the yellow pages of your phone directory.)

Aerial Photograph

PRODUCT NAMES

Verbal **fluency** and **word choice** get a big workout when a writer is asked to name a product.

DIRECTIONS:

1. On the board, write a type of product or a store that sells a particular product. Be as specific as possible, for example, a *24-hour donut shop* rather than just *donut shop*. (See following page for additional subjects to name.)

2. Have students brainstorm words and phrases that come to mind when thinking about the product or store.

3. Students then list as many original names as they can for the product or store. Naming categories include:
   - Alliterative words—Terrific Toys
   - Noises—The Boom Bang Drum Shop
   - Puns—Curl Up and Dye (beauty salon)
   - Rhymes—Deals on Wheels (bike store)

4. Each student picks a favorite name and writes a sentence explaining what makes the name special.

EXTENSION:

Have students write to companies asking about the origins of well-known product or store names. They can turn the results of this research into a book.

Products and Stores to Name

automobile that runs on electricity

barber shop

bicycle shop

bookstore

bubble gum

clothing store for kids

computer

eyeglasses that let people see in the dark

glass shop (sells windows for cars and homes)

hardware shop

ice cream shop

joke shop

kite shop

laundromat

magic shop

marbles

model train store

one-hour photo shop

package wrapping store

pen that writes under water

pet shop just for _____ (cats, dogs, birds)

playground equipment store

popcorn

shoe store

sports store

television sales and repair store

toy store

travel agency

umbrella

video rental shop

wristwatch

PUNCTUATION HUNT

One way to master **punctuation** is to pay attention to punctuation marks as they appear in context.

DIRECTIONS:
1. Find or write a passage that contains several punctuation marks studied in class. Number each line and make copies for each student or pair of students.
2. On the board, list the marks that you want the students to look for.
3. Have students, working in pairs, read the passage, discuss each mark, and—on a separate sheet of paper—explain why the mark was used. For example:

   line 6—An exclamation mark is used to show feeling.

   line 8—A comma is used between things in a list.

EXTENSION:
Have students dress up in punctuation costumes and give speeches about the different marks.

QUESTIONS AND CONVERSATIONS

The process of dreaming up interesting **questions** plays a central role in reading comprehension, conversation, writing, and other language activities.

DIRECTIONS:
1. Divide the class into pairs.
2. Present an interesting painting, photograph, or illustration from a picture book. The art should feature a strong subject such as a character or event. A good example is "Whistler's Mother."
3. Have students brainstorm open-ended questions about the subject, for example, "Why would you like—or not like—this person to be your teacher?" Or: "What might make you think that this person is—or isn't—a criminal?"
4. Have students ask their questions and then listen to the responses of other students.

EXTENSION:
Students can brainstorm factual questions about the picture, and then can research the answers.

"RADIO" READERS

Students' **listening** skills will improve when they hear tape recordings that evoke old-time radio broadcasts.

DIRECTIONS:
1. Ahead of time, have a variety of readers, including other teachers and older students, practice and then record a short story, a poem, or an article. Longer works can be serialized—broken into segments of five or ten minutes.
2. Play the "radio" readings in class. To set the old-time mood, dim the lights.

EXTENSION:
Dedicate one entire "radio" series to student-written work. It's a real treat for writers to hear their work read aloud by good readers. As a related project, arrange for your students to produce their own radio readings for playback in other classrooms.

READING RELAY

Reading comprehension requires students to read smoothly from one sentence to the next. However, to help students avoid "run-on writing," the following **responsive reading** activity clarifies the fact that every story or article consists of separate **sentences**.

DIRECTIONS:
1. Divide the class into pairs.
2. Give each pair a short reading consisting of at least eight or ten sentences.
3. Have the pairs quietly read aloud their passages, alternating at sentence breaks.

EXTENSION:
Do the same activity, but have the readers alternate at paragraph breaks.

RELATED WORDS

Thoughtful speakers and writers pay attention to the
small but important differences between related words.
Such awareness leads to more thoughtful **word choice**.

DIRECTIONS:
1. List a pair of related words on the board, for example,
skip and *jump*. (See following page for additional pairs.)
2. Ask students, working in groups of two or three, to
talk about how the words are alike and different. For
example:

> Skipping and jumping are both words about moving.
> Skipping is a kind of running. You go someplace.
> Jumping is more an up-and-down way to move.

3. Have students write one or two sentences illustrating
the meaning of the words:

> When I was frightened, I jumped up.
> I was so happy, I skipped all the way to school.

4. The small groups can share their insights with the
entire class orally or on the board.

EXTENSION:
Have students create a related-words dictionary.

A chair is a piece of furniture that you sit on. It has four legs and a back.

A stool is like a chair but it doesn't have a back.

Related Words

argue/talk
baby/child
borrow/take
broken/destroyed
build/make
cage/prison
chair/stool
circle/wheel
clock/watch
cold/freezing
cry/whine
cut/rip
damp/wet
dirty/messy
dream/sleep
drink/water
drizzle/rain
eat/gulp
evening/night
find/discover
glass/window
hit/smash
hold/squeeze
hole/opening
hot/warm
jog/race
lake/river
laugh/smile
mix/shake
see/stare
small/tiny
swim/splash
think/wonder

RETOLD STORIES

William Shakespeare, Walt Disney, and other storytellers based their hits on borrowed tales. Retelling (adapting) a story teaches many literary skills, including **plotting** and **character development**.

DIRECTIONS:
1. While reading aloud a short story, a children's picture book, a chapter from a novel, a narrative poem, or an article that tells a true story, encourage students to imagine or draw what they hear.
2. Divide the class into pairs.
3. Ask students to tell the story to each other in their own words, making changes in characters or the setting. Or have students write their own versions.

EXTENSION:
Have students write stories based on movies or TV shows. Professionals call these retold stories "novelizations."

SENSATIONAL SENTENCES

According to many writers, the predicate is the key to powerful **sentence writing**. The predicate, which includes the verb, gives the news about the subject.

DIRECTIONS:
1. Write the subject for a sentence on the board. For example:

   A cat ———————————————————.

2. Have students complete the sentence in as many ways as they can. The completed sentences can be silly or serious. Challenge students to come up with sentence enders that no one else will think of.
3. Have students share their predicates.

EXTENSION:
Have each student choose a favorite completed sentence and write a story or essay using it as the lead sentence.

SENTENCE EXPANDING

To make a point, often a simple statement works best: "Keep off the grass." Other times, a **detail-rich sentence** is the ticket: "Please do not walk on what may look like mud to you but is really the beginning of our new lawn."

DIRECTIONS:

1. Write a simple sentence on the board, dividing it into the subject and the predicate. For example:

> The jetliner
> flies.

(See following page for additional sentences.)

2. Have students work in pairs to add details to both parts:

> The giant, four-engine Northwest jetliner
> flies above the skyscrapers toward the clouds.

3. Share the expanded sentences orally or on the board. Discuss the different images created through the use of different details.

EXTENSION:

Have students give each other simple sentences for expanding.

Simple Sentences for Expanding

I know how to fly a kite.

My friend enjoys math.

That building burned down.

Reading is fun.

Lightning can be dangerous.

The shark chased me.

Three friends want to sing.

Bring me a sandwich.

The television isn't working.

I waited an hour for you.

The phone rang twice.

Sandy planted tomato seeds.

Jack and Jill went up the hill.

Those people look happy.

The stranger talked.

The painting is beautiful.

That noise kept me awake.

Here comes the dog.

Lunch is ready.

My cousin likes spinach.

The baby can crawl.

The spider is spinning a web.

My book got muddy.

The child went into the kitchen.

Music makes me want to dance.

The mirror got broken.

SENTENCE LINKING

Good writers and readers pay attention to how one sentence connects with the next. Carefully planned **sentence linking** makes for a smooth flow of ideas.

DIRECTIONS:

1. On the board, write a detail-rich sentence. For example:

   This evening, a storm might drop six inches of snow on our town.

2. Tell students to write a follow-up sentence that uses at least one key word or phrase from the starting sentence. For example:

   Six inches of snow is enough to cause a very big traffic jam.

3. Students continue chaining sentences this way until time runs out. Thus, a third sentence might be:

   One winter, my family was caught in a horrible *traffic jam* caused by a heavy snowfall.

4. Have students share their sentences with their partners.

EXTENSION:

Have students look for links between sentences published in books, newspapers, or magazines. Usually, words won't be repeated in the two sentences, but the connections should still be clear. For example, in the example below *friend* links with *he*, and *present* links with *it*:

   My friend gave me a present. He knew I would like it.

SENTENCE SHOPPING

Good writing is often characterized by **sentence variety.** This means using all sorts of sentences—long ones and short ones; statements, questions, and commands.

DIRECTIONS:

1. Choose a piece of writing that has a variety of sentence types.
2. Give students a "shopping list" of examples to find:

   A. Find the shortest and the longest sentences.
   B. Find a sentence with a compound (double) subject.
   C. Find a sentence with two verbs.

3. Have students share their discoveries in small groups.

EXTENSION:

Students paraphrase the sentences in a literary model such as a picture book or a poem.

SENTENCE SLICING

Writers package some ideas in chunks—phrases and clauses—rather than in single words. Learning to recognize verbal chunks helps improve **reading comprehension**.

DIRECTIONS:
1. Write a sentence on the board. The sentence can come from a story or newspaper article, or it might be a proverb. (See Resources.)
2. Have students slice the sentence into several meaningful chunks and then stack the chunks in a list. For example, here's one sliced and stacked version of the first sentence on this page:

> Writers package
> some ideas
> in chunks—
> phrases and clauses—
> rather than in single words.

Just as different musicians may interpret the same piece differently, different readers may find different chunks in a given sentence:

> Writers
> package
> some ideas
> in chunks—
> phrases and clauses—
> rather than
> in single words.

3. Students can share their sliced sentences on the board.

EXTENSION:
Have students create poem-like works (called "found poems") by slicing paragraphs from books or newspapers.

SENTENCE SWAPPING

While **drafting** a piece, experienced writers sometimes stop and read over what they have just written. This makes for stronger **transitions** and more unified **paragraphs**.

DIRECTIONS:
1. Have each student think up a topic that every other person in the room will know something about, for example, getting dressed.
2. Students each write a single sentence that starts a paper or story about their topics.
3. Have students switch papers with a partner.
4. The partner now reads the sentence and adds a sentence that continues the thought.
5. Continue swapping back and forth until time runs out.
6. Have students read aloud the work in small groups.

EXTENSION:
Try the same activity with longer pieces. In this case, students will swap papers after completing paragraphs.

SHRINKING STORIES

Writing synopses is a study skill that applies to all subject areas. This **summarizing** activity also provides practice in finding the main idea and in writing concisely.

DIRECTIONS:
1. Prepare a short (100-word) passage from a newspaper, magazine, or book. Alternatively, you might have students choose their own readings.
2. Students carefully read the material. They may underline important passages or take notes.
3. After the reading, students write their own versions using 25 words or less. The goal is to include only the most important facts and ideas.
4. The synopses can be shared in small groups or posted.

EXTENSION:
Have students write synopses of favorite TV shows. Another option is to create a weekly "news round-up" bulletin board with each student contributing a synopsis of an article in the newspaper.

SIMPLY PUT

One of the best **reading comprehension** practices is to translate material into simpler terms.

DIRECTIONS:
1. Give students a short passage written at grade level: an excerpt from a text or library book, a poem, a proverb, a fable, or a familiar piece such as "The Pledge of Allegiance."
2. Have students rewrite the selection so that children two or three years younger might understand it. Suggest that sentences be kept short and that "big" words be defined in context or with simpler synonyms.

EXTENSION:
Have students test their simplified pieces by sharing them with the intended readers.

SPELLING TRICKS

English spelling is not always logical. For example, since there's a *u* in *four*, why isn't there a *u* in *forty?* And why *is* there a *d* in *Wednesday?* With nutty words like these, inventing memory tricks can promote correct **spelling**.

DIRECTIONS:
1. For a week or two before doing this activity, have students list frequently misspelled words on chart paper.
2. Ask students to choose a word they wish to learn how to spell. Working with partners, students write a sentence with a simple clue to remind them of the correct spelling. (See next page for model spelling tricks.)
3. Students may wish to illustrate their clues for additional memory support.

EXTENSION:
Collect the memory tricks into a class book so that other students can use them when needed. Consider placing a copy of the book in the school library.

Spelling Tricks

1. Word-within-a-word Clue

   I p**aid** for first **aid**.
   Al a**l**ways smiles.
   Hide from a **hide**ous monster.

2. Shared-letter(s) Clue

   The b**ea**ch is by the s**ea**.

3. Related-word Clue

   If you have **musc**les, you are **musc**ular.

4. Descriptive-statement Clue

   You will be doubly embarrassed if you miss the two
   double letters in emba**rr**a**ss**ed.

5. Two-word Clue

   All right (two words) is the opposite of **all wrong** (two
   words).

   High school (two words) comes after **elementary
   school** (two words).

6. Mispronunciation Clue

   Pronounce "Wednesday" as "Wed Nes Day."

7. Silly-sentence Clue (linking similarly spelled words)

   The boo**kk**eeper lost hear ea**rr**ings but the hitc**hh**iker
   found them.

8. Combination Clues (two different clues in one
sentence)

   A **missile** shouldn't **miss** by a m**ile**.

STAND-IN WORDS

According to Mark Twain, "The difference between the right word and the almost right word is like the difference between lightning and the lightning bug." The idea is that writers must be careful about **word choice**.

DIRECTIONS:
1. On the board, write a word that has at least several obvious synonyms, for example, *big*.
2. Have students, working alone or with partners, list three or four words or phrases that mean about the same thing, for example: *large, enormous, tall, fat, giant*.
3. Students now write sentences to illustrate the slightly different meanings of the similar words.

EXTENSION:
Create a class thesaurus.

Big   Tall   Giant   Fat

STOP-N-CROP

Because there isn't time to tell everything, writers often concentrate on just a part of a subject. The following activity provides practice in **narrowing the focus**.

DIRECTIONS:
1. Find a large picture that the whole class can see. Or give each student a different picture. (Good sources are magazine covers.)
2. Have each student write a few sentences about the whole picture.
3. Next, have students draw an outline around a small part of the picture, and then write the same amount of words about that portion.
4. Share the writing in small groups.

EXTENSION:
Choose a large time period, for example, summer vacation. Then have students write about a very short period within the larger time period, for example, "An Hour That I'll Always Remember from Last Summer." Make a book of these memorable moments.

TELEPHONE "NUMBERS"

As a memory aid, many companies think up verbal phone numbers. A travel agent might tell clients to phone 1-800-GETAWAY. **Brainstorming** these "numbers" is a fun way to boost interest in **word choice**.

DIRECTIONS:
1. Choose an occupation or company that might use a creative phone number. (See next page for examples.)
2. Have students, working alone or in small groups, generate as many "numbers" as possible. For example, names for an umbrella shop might include:

    1-800-STAYDRY
    1-800-KEEPDRY
    1-800-NODROPS
    1-800-PROTECT
    1-800-LIFTTOP

3. Have each student or student team choose one number and explain in a sentence why it's the best.

EXTENSION:
Create a class book of zany phone numbers for storybook characters, famous people, and well-known groups or businesses.

Phone Customer List

art museum
art supply store
baby shop
bakery
bicycle shop
bookstore
bus depot
cab company
candy shop
clothing store
dentist
dry cleaner
electrician
exterminator
gas station
hospital
ice cream store
laundry
library
movie theater
NASA
pet shop
pharmacy
pizzeria
plumber
roller rink
shoe store
supermarket
toy store
travel agency
veterinarian
video shop

TERRIFIC TITLES

Often, students give little thought to the titles of their writing. That's unfortunate. A working title can help the writer focus on the **main idea**. And the final title can draw a reader's attention to the piece.

DIRECTIONS:
1. For a week prior to introducing this activity, have students bring in examples of different types of titles. (See the following page for examples.) The titles can come from books, movies, television shows, or songs.
2. Have students pick a topic that they know a lot about, for example, a hobby, a good friend, a room at home, a favorite vacation spot, or a sport.
3. Ask students, working in pairs, to write four or five different types of titles that might be used for a piece about their chosen topics. Encourage them to include details in the titles. For example, "The Angry Ocean" is more interesting than "The Ocean."
4. Have students get feedback on their titles from others in the class.

EXTENSION:
Take a trip to the library and have students look for examples of different types of titles. Make a bulletin board that presents their findings.

Types of Titles

Activities or Events
- *Alexander's Midnight Snack*
- *Bill and Pete Go Down the Nile*
- *Dream of the Little Elephant*
- *Redhawk's Account of Custer's Last Battle*

Characters
- *Frog Prince*
- *One Hungry Monster*
- *Tales of a Fourth Grade Nothing*
- *Tuck Everlasting*

Commands
- *Ask Mr. Bear*
- *Escape If You Can*
- *Move Over, Mother Goose*
- *Never Snap at a Bubble*
- *Use Your Head, Dear*

Objects
- *Bear's Bicycle*
- *Charlotte's Web*
- *The 500 Hats of Bartholomew Cubbins*
- *Pig and the Magic Photo Album*

Places
- *Bear in the Bathtub*
- *Charlie and the Chocolate Factory*
- *Rabbit on Bear Mountain*
- *There's a Monster in My Closet*
- *Where the Wild Things Are*

Problems
- *Bear's Toothache*
- *The Cat Ate My Gymsuit*
- *Too Many Monsters*

Questions
- *Are You Forgetting Something, Fiona?*
- *Are You There, Baby Bear?*

Sounds
- *Ah-Choo*

Times
- *The Day the Teacher Went Bananas*
- *Night*
- *Snowy Day*
- *Up Day Down Day*

THANK YOU, FAIRY GODMOTHER

Writing a thank-you note involves **descriptive writing** and, of course, good manners.

DIRECTIONS:
1. Have students pick a storybook character who should write a thank-you note. You might present a list of candidates, for example:
- Cinderella—thanks her Fairy Godmother
- First two little pigs—thank the third little pig
- Little Red Riding Hood—thanks the Woodchopper

2. Each student writes a thank-you note that describes the gift or favor and explains why it's valued.
3. If there is time, students can share their notes in small groups.

EXTENSION:
Have students write book reports in the form of a thank-you note from one character to another. Another option is writing and sending thank-you notes to helpful members of the school staff such as the secretary, the janitor, or the librarian.

THERE'S NO "NOISE" IN ILLINOIS

Writing memory tricks for correct **pronunciation** can spark a deeper interest in words. It also promotes confidence when students face public speaking and other oral language challenges.

DIRECTIONS:
1. Make sure every student or student team has a dictionary.
2. List a tricky-to-pronounce (or often mispronounced) word on the board, for example, *Illinois*.
3. Have the students look up the word, figure out how to pronounce it, and then write a sentence or two that gives a clue about how to pronounce the word. For example:

> There's no noise in Illinois. The last letter is silent. The right way to say the word is "Ill in oy."

4. Have students share their pronunciation tips orally in small groups or write them on the board.

EXTENSION:
Make a book of pronunciation tips. For a model, see Charles Elster's witty *There's No Zoo in Zoology* (Collier, 1988).

Pronunciation Puzzlers

Note: Some words have more than one acceptable pronunciation.

asked

Arkansas

athlete

cafe

catsup

cement

colonel

Connecticut

debt

debut

etc.

fasten

February

film

forbade

genuine

government

herb

Illinois

interesting

island

library

often

pneumonia

sandwich

valet

THOSE ARE THE BREAKS

To make writing easier to understand, writers use **indenting** to break their work into **paragraphs**. Some paragraphing rules are followed by all careful writers, for example: "Start a new paragraph each time a different person begins to speak." Other paragraph decisions are a matter of style.

DIRECTIONS:
1. Type a short story or a short passage from a story the students are reading, leaving out all paragraph indentations. Number the lines to make later discussion easier. Make a copy for each student or pair of students.
2. Have students read the manuscript and use the paragraph symbol (¶) to indicate paragraph breaks.
3. Next, have students compare the breaks they proposed with those in the original. Discuss any discrepancies. Invite students to explain their choices.

EXTENSION:
Have students create "find the paragraphs" worksheets for each other.

A new character is talking here, so we need a new paragraph.

UNCOMMON SENSING

Descriptive writing begins with keen **observation**. By sharpening their senses, students lay the foundation for creating fresher and more accurate stories, reports, and other assignments.

DIRECTIONS:
1. Show an everyday object or a picture of an object.
2. Students, working in pairs, list as many sensory words as they can that describe the object:

  Desk: hard, smooth, brown
  Bicycle handlebars: smooth, curved, shiny

3. Have students share their lists with the whole class. Discuss which words are most descriptive.

EXTENSION:
Have students use sensory details to describe a place, for example, a room at home or a setting from a book.

WHAT NEXT?

Reading comprehension requires an active, rather than a passive, attitude. **Predicting** what happens in the next part of a story or article is a classic activity.

DIRECTIONS:
1. While reading a story, poem, or article to the class, stop and ask students to discuss in small groups what they think comes next.
2. Bring the class together and list on the board some or all of the predictions. Ask students to give reasons for their predictions. Emphasize that having a reasonable explanation for the prediction is more important than getting the prediction "right."
3. Read the next passage. Students should compare their predictions with the actual text. Each student can privately decide which version is "better."

EXTENSION:
Have students write and illustrate "new" fairy tales, fables, or picture books by substituting their own endings for those found in the originals.

WHAT'S IN A NAME?

Reading comprehension starts with the cover of the book. This means **predicting** the contents by thinking about the title.

DIRECTIONS:
1. Find a descriptively-titled picture book that your class is likely to be unfamiliar with, for example, *The Boy Who Was Followed Home* or *The Amazing Bone*. (Try recently published works.)
2. Write the title on the board and have the students try to predict what the book is about. They might even draw pictures that predict key scenes. Point out that you value imaginative predictions, whether or not they prove to be "correct." Indeed, a student's prediction might be more interesting than what happens in the actual book.
3. Read the book. If there's time—or later on—have students discuss their predictions.

EXTENSION:
Do the same activity with a longer book that has descriptive chapter titles. Before reading each chapter, invite students to predict the content based on the chapter title.

WORD CHASE

One key to **vocabulary building** is discovering that one word can lead to another and another and...

DIRECTIONS:
1. Have each student or student team choose a starting word, for example, *house*.
2. Ask students to look up the word in the dictionary and write down its main (or first) definition. For example:

> *house*, a building in which a group of people live.

3. Students now choose one of the words in the definition—for example, *live*—and write its definition under the first one.
4. Students continue the sequence, seeing how many words they can look up in ten minutes.

EXTENSION:
Play the game without a dictionary. Create a series of definitions, chaining one to the next:

> An alarm clock wakens a person from sleep.
> Sleep is rest for the mind and body.
> A body is the main part of a person or animal.
> An animal is a living thing that can move by itself.

WORD PREVIEWS

One of the best **vocabulary building** strategies is to pay attention to words in context.

Ahead of time, choose a passage that contains two or three words that will be new to most of the class. Sources include poems, stories, articles, or textbooks.

DIRECTIONS:

1. On the board, write the words that students should listen for.
2. Read the passage aloud.
3. Divide the class into small groups and have students in each group discuss the meanings of the words listed.
4. Read aloud the dictionary's definition of each word so that students can evaluate their context-based insights. Be sure to point out that the meaning of most words depends a lot on how the words are used.

EXTENSION:

Have students deliver "word preview" book reports. The report maker focuses on a few important words when talking about the book. The words should be presented in context. As a bonus, the student might provide information about the words' etymologies.

"Dorothy saw the tornado coming."

In the story I'm going to read, you will hear this word—tornado. It's a storm with whirling winds. The word comes from a Spanish word meaning "to turn."

Tornado

WORD ROOTS

Tracing related words back to a common root is a key to **vocabulary building**. It also gives practice in using the dictionary.

DIRECTIONS:
1. Write two or more related words on the board. (See next page for examples.)
2. Students use a dictionary to locate the root common to the words. For example, *astronaut* and *disaster* both come from the Latin word *aster,* meaning "star."
3. Have each student write a single sentence that uses both words and underline the letters that the words have in common. For example:

   A<u>st</u>ronauts work carefully to avoid a di<u>ast</u>er in space.

4. Share the sentences orally or on a bulletin board.

EXTENSION:
Create a class book of related words.

Root-sharing Words

apron/napkin
astronaut/disaster
attract/tractor
autograph/automobile
automobile/mob
balloon/ballot
bank/bench
Bible/bibliography
biscuit/bicycle
captain/capitol
companion/company
congregate/Congress
December/decimal
Egypt/gypsy
frigid/refrigerator
geography/telegraph
legal/logical

lens/lentil
manufacture/manual
marine/submarine
member/remember
month/moon
mouse/muscle
nose/nostril
October/octopus
pasta/paste
police/politics
portable/report
secret/secretary
sign/signal
telephone/television
thermometer/thermos
two/twin
vital/vitamin

WRITE BY THE CLOCK

Free (or quick) writing is a **fluency** activity that can improve **drafting** skills.

DIRECTIONS:
1. Choose a topic that students know a lot about, for example, swimming or hamsters. (See following page for additional topics.)
2. Have students write on that topic for a set amount of time, for example, three minutes. The only rule is that each student's pencil or pen keep moving for the entire time. For example:

> I know how to make great paper airplanes. I've done it for years. But I can't think of anything to say about it. My mind is as blank as a sheet of paper. Speaking of paper, I like to make paper airplanes using paper with writing on it. They look unusual when they soar through the air carrying words. A spelling test works well. Or maybe my math homework...

EXTENSION:
Have students use their quick-writing material as a starting point for a polished story or article.

Topics for Quick Writing

Animals: What animal would you choose to be and why?

Book: What is your favorite book and why?

Gifts: What's the best gift you ever gave? What made it so good?

Invisible: If you could make yourself invisible, how would you use that power?

Movie: Describe your favorite movie or TV show.

Object: What object would you choose to be and why?

People: If you could be another person, who would it be and why?

Possession: If you could own anything in the world that you don't now have, what would it be? Why would you want it?

Problem: What problem would you most like to see solved? Why?

Skill: What skill do you have that you most value? Describe how you learned that skill.

Words: List three words that are important to you. Pick one and explain why it's important.

Work: If you could do any job in the world, what would it be and why?

Yourself: If you could meet yourself at any other age, what age would you choose and why?

How would you describe yourself to someone who had never met you?

What do you like best about yourself?

YOU STORIES

An unusual way to involve readers is to put them right into a story. This can be done by using the second person **point of view**.

DIRECTIONS:

1. Pick a short, familiar story and list the main characters on the board. For example, with "Little Red Riding Hood," you'd list Little Red Riding Hood, the wolf, and the Woodchopper.

2. Have each student choose one of the characters and briefly rewrite the story by talking directly to the chosen character. For example:

   You are planning to take a basket of goodies to your grandmother...

3. Have students share their stories with their partners.

EXTENSION:

Have students write original "you stories" based on experiences they have had, for example, getting a flat tire on a bicycle, or having the dentist drill a tooth.

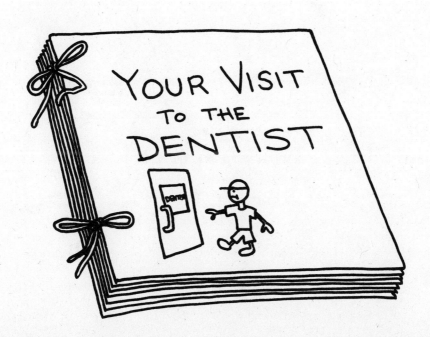

YOUR WORDS ARE MY WORDS

Most of us are better at **listening** when our conversation partner is speaking about something that interests us.

DIRECTIONS:
1. Ask students to list five words they think everyone in the room knows something about.
2. Divide the class into pairs.
3. Have each student choose a word from the partner's list and talk about it for a couple of minutes. The partner should then feel free to add a comment.
4. Reverse roles.

EXTENSION:
Students write stories or articles based on a word borrowed from a partner.

ONGOING PRACTICES

The following activities can be integrated into the regular routines of your whole language classroom, for example, sustained silent reading. These ideas are meant to add richness to the practices and to provide variety for each of the standard strategies.

Reading Aloud

Technicolor Reading: Have students choose a favorite paragraph (one that can be read in three minutes) from their sustained silent reading book. Give time for each student to practice reading aloud. You might list—and demonstrate—some characteristics of effective oral reading, for example:
- Read smoothly.
- Group words together into meaningful chunks, rather than give isolated words equal emphasis.
- Vary the speed and volume according to the passage.
- Make eye contact.
- Enunciate clearly.
- Pay attention to pronunciation. When unsure, check the dictionary or ask someone for help.
- Sometimes use a facial or body gesture for emphasis, but don't overdo it.

Then have students read for each other and give each other specific feedback. As an extension, sometimes arrange for students to tape-record their readings.

Story Sequencing: After you read a story aloud, on the board write the episodes in random order. In small groups, students sequence the episodes. For a more challenging activity, have students change the sequence and/or add information to create a new story.

In One Ear and Out the Mouth: After reading aloud a chapter from a book or an article, divide the class into pairs and have students retell the passage to each other. Listening to the retellings will allow you to check student comprehension.

Impending Events: At a key point in a read-aloud session, stop and ask students to discuss with a partner what they think will happen next. Have a few students briefly share their predictions.

Sustained Silent Reading

Reading Graphs: Each day, have students record the type of literature they have just read during sustained silent reading: poetry, fiction, nonfiction, humor, or whatever. Once a week, graph the results.

Quick Critic: After a sustained silent reading session, have each student write a one-sentence opinion of the passage just read. If there's time, students can share their opinions in small groups. Teach students to write more than just "I liked it" by encouraging them to comment on characters, plot, description, or style.

Vocabulary Word of the Day

Headline Words: Find and discuss a word that appears in a newspaper headline. Older students can take turns choosing and presenting these important headline expressions.

Word Origins: Read aloud brief etymologies of words that might interest your students or that would enrich an area of study, for example, Greek myths. You can find these stories in etymological dictionaries available in most libraries and bookstores.

Phrase Meanings: Introduce students to a familiar phrase or idiom, for example, "to hit the nail on the head." A handy reference is Charles Funk's *A Hog on Ice*.

Literature Study

What's So Funny?: Have students read aloud a joke or a silly poem by a witty writer such as Shel Silverstein. Discuss with the students what makes the piece funny. Topics to explore include:
- puns (deliberately mixing up homonyms)
- unexpected behavior
- surprising point of view

Chunk It: After silent reading, orally model for the students the chunks of meaning and intonation of a particular passage. Then have the students read the passage together as a choral reading.

Whole Class Lessons

Model Editing: At a time when students have completed drafts of stories, reports, poems, or whatever, guide them through an editing session looking for a particular element. Using an overhead projector, demonstrate how you edit your own work. For example, think aloud as you check for quotation marks. Then encourage the students to do the same thing with their papers.

Echo Teaching: During a whole-group lesson, divide the class into pairs and ask students to take turns teaching each other what they have learned so far.

All That Glitters: After showing a film or video, or reading a story, have students list all the details they can remember. They then identify the most important idea and discuss what makes it so important.

Learning Log: At the end of a lesson, have students write in their journals brief summaries of what they learned. Questions should be included as well. On a regular basis, have students review their learning logs and pose their questions to their classmates and to you.

Reading Speeds: An important reading comprehension strategy is adjusting the speed of reading to the type of material. Practice this skill by giving texts that require different reading rates. Coach students by saying something like "Read this paragraph slowly" or "Skim through this material."

Whole Language at a Glance

IT IS...

Integrated

Reading, writing, speaking, and listening are used and developed together. They are interdependent.

Student-centered

Activities often originate with students' interests. Lessons are taught when students need them. Students are encouraged to self-evaluate.

Interdisciplinary

The language arts are processes used for learning in all curriculum areas, just as they are used in the world of adult work. Content lines may blur as a particular theme is investigated.

Authentic

Students are involved in "real-world" (whole) projects with real audiences. Reading-oriented projects tend to deal with literature created for the whole person rather than expressly for students; the emphasis is on picture books, novels, short stories, nonfiction books, poetry, magazine articles, and so on.

Active

Students are active learners. They are invited to make decisions, to create their own meanings, to take responsibility for their learning and behavior, to ask questions, and to share their knowledge with peers, younger and older students, and people outside of school.

IT IS NOT...

Fragmented

The language arts are treated as separate subjects.

Curriculum-centered

Activities often originate in curriculum materials with pre-set goals and outcomes. Ability groups are used and evaluation is seen as a teacher task.

Content-isolated

Language is handled as a discipline separate from other parts of the curriculum.

Artificial

Priority is given to completing worksheets or workbook pages. Textbooks are the primary source of information and the major stimuli for language arts activities.

Passive

Students are required to be quiet, to do as they are told, to listen, to do their worksheets, and to memorize, with the goal of performing well on paper-and-pencil tests.

IT IS...

Process-based

The language arts are modeled and practiced daily. Students learn about a task, practice it, and then get encouraging feedback. Skills are taught in context.

In a whole language classroom, students may be binding books, conducting polls, building models, doing interviews, or comparing lab reports. A major teaching goal is to develop challenging projects that build self-esteem.

Collaborative

Because language is primarily a social tool, students have many opportunities to function in a variety of small, heterogeneous groups. At different times, the groups have different purposes: sharing ideas, practicing new skills, working on activities, or solving problems. Student talk is important.

Motivation is intrinsic. For example, a student picture-book author gets the satisfaction of watching a younger child read the completed picture book.

Multi-media

While the written word has a unique place in our culture, language can be developed by giving students opportunities to use all their senses and to use many tools, such as tape recorders, cameras, and overhead projectors.

In addition to writing, students will create a wide variety of audio-visual works including posters, photographs, puppet shows, videotapes, audiotapes, bulletin boards, posters, plays, and songs.

IT IS NOT...

Sub-skills based

Skills are practiced out of context. Feedback takes the form of letter or number grades rather than meaningful comments.

Competitive

Most activities are solo, with instruction usually moving in one direction—from teacher to students. Students are compared to each other by star charts, grades, and ability groups. Extrinsic motivational principles are used. Having a quiet classroom is considered a plus; students who talk may be seen as cheating.

Print-dominated

Language activities focus almost entirely on reading and writing.

Children's Literature and Language Skills

A good way to introduce any concept is to present an example. You may want to refer to *Using Picture Storybooks to Teach Literary Devices* by Susan Hall (Oryx Press, 1990). Here is a sampler of books that serve effectively as introductory readings.

ADJECTIVES

A Is for Angry by Sandra Boynton (Workman, 1983)

ALLITERATION

All About Arthur (An Absolutely Absurd Ape) by Eric Carle (Watts, 1974)

Alphabet Annie Announces an All-American Album by Marcia O'Shell and Susan Purviance (Houghton Mifflin, 1988)

AUTOBIOGRAPHY

Homesick: My Own Story by Jean Fritz (Putnam, 1982)

Self-Portrait by Trina Schart Hyman (Harper, 1981)

When I Was Young in the Mountains by Cynthia Rylant (Dutton, 1982)

COMPOUND WORDS

Puniddles by Bruce McMillan (Houghton Mifflin, 1982)

HOMONYMS

In a Pickle by Marvin Terban (Clarion, 1983)

A Little Pigeon Toad by Fred Gwynne (Simon & Schuster, 1988)

What a Tale by Brian Wildsmith (Oxford, 1986)

Your Ant Is a Which by Bernice Kohn Hunt (Harcourt, 1975)

IDIOMS

Punching the Clock by Marvin Terban (Clarion, 1990)

JOURNALS

Gathering of Days by Joan Blos (Scribner, 1979)

Harriet the Spy by Louise Fitzhugh (Harper, 1964)

On the Frontier with Mr. Audubon by Barbara Breer (Coward, 1977)

LETTER WRITING

C.S. Lewis' Letters to Children by C.S. Lewis (Macmillan, 1985)

Dear Mr. Henshaw by Beverly Cleary (Dell, 1983)

The Jolly Postman by Janet and Allan Ahlberg (Little Brown, 1986)

OBSERVING

Do You See What I See? by Matthew Price and Sue Porter (Harper, 1986)

If at First You Do Not See by Ruth Brown (Holt, 1982)

Look Again by Tana Hoban (Macmillan, 1971)

POINT OF VIEW

Ben and Me by Robert Lawson (Little, Brown, 1934)

The True Story of the Three Little Pigs by A. Wolf by Jon Scieszka (Viking, 1989)

Two Bad Ants by Chris Van Allsburg (Houghton Mifflin, 1988)

PREPOSITIONAL PHRASES

Rosie's Walk by Pat Hutchins (Macmillan, 1968)

PRONUNCIATION

Tongue Twisters and Tricky Tanglers by Duncan Emrich (Scholastic, 1975)

RIDDLES

A Mad Wet Hen and Other Riddles by Joseph Low (Greenwillow, 1977)

SENTENCE EXPANDING

Animalia by Graeme Base (Abrams, 1987)

STORYTELLING & STORY WRITING

The Day Jimmy's Boa Ate the Wash by Trinka Hakes
Noble (Dial, 1980)

The Frog Prince Continued by Jon Scieszka (Viking,
1991)

Nothing Much Happened Today by Mary Blount
Christian (Addison-Wesley, 1973)

VERBS

A to Z by Sandra Boynton (Simon & Schuster, 1990)

Adelaide to Zeke by Janet Wolf (Harper, 1987)

I Think I Thought and Other Tricky Verbs by Marvin
Terban (Houghton Mifflin, 1984)

Kites Sail High by Ruth Heller (Grosset & Dunlap,
1988)

VOCABULARY

A Hole Is to Dig by Ruth Krauss (Harper, 1952)

Follow the Line by Demi (Holt, 1981)

Guppies in Tuxedos: Funny Eponyms by Marvin
Terban (Clarion, 1988)

What's a Frank Frank? by Giulio Maestro (Clarion,
1984)

Fables

The following fables may be used with NOTE CARD OUTLINE, PARAPHRASING, SIMPLY PUT and other activities that spring from short readings.

The Fox and the Grapes
A fox came upon a huge vine of beautiful grapes. Unfortunately, the grapes grew only near the top of the vine. When the fox realized that he could not reach the delicious-looking fruit, he said to himself, "These grapes are probably sour. I wouldn't like them even if I could get them."

Moral: We often say something is no good when we know we can't have it.

The Ant and the Grasshopper
During the entire summer, the grasshopper sang and played and had all kinds of fun. Meanwhile, the hard-working ant tended its garden, growing many vegetables and other good things to eat.

When winter came, the grasshopper became hungry. Because it had gathered no food, the grasshopper went to the ant and begged for something to eat. But the ant replied, "You were silly to spend your whole summer singing. Now you must dance on an empty stomach."

Moral: A wise person plans for the future.

The Milkmaid's Chickens
A milkmaid was walking along with a pitcher of fresh milk. She talked to herself about what she would do with the milk: "I'll churn it into butter. Then I'll trade the butter for some eggs. The eggs will hatch into chickens. The chickens will lay more eggs. Soon I'll have hundreds and thousands of chickens and eggs to sell and I'll be rich."

The milkmaid was so caught up in her thinking that she didn't watch her step. She tripped and spilled all the milk and ended up with no chickens and no eggs.

Moral: Don't count your chickens before they hatch.

The Lion and the Mouse

A lion, who had been awakened by a mouse, was so angry that he threatened to kill the mouse. The mouse pleaded, "If you let me live, maybe someday I will be able to do a favor for you."

The lion, who was so much bigger and stronger than the mouse, laughed at this idea. But he decided to let the mouse live and he allowed it to run away.

Soon after, the lion became tangled in a hunter's trap. But before the hunter returned, the very same mouse came by, saw the lion, and nibbled through the rope that bound him.

Moral: We all have the ability to help each other.

The Fox and the Crow

A crow, which had just found a piece of cheese, flew to the top of a tree where it planned to enjoy a snack.

A fox that came by desired the cheese, but it didn't know how to climb the tree. Then it got an idea and said aloud, "I'll bet that crow up there has a beautiful voice."

The crow, wanting to show off, opened its mouth and began to sing. But as soon as it did, the cheese fell down and the fox pounced on it.

While eating the cheese, the fox called up to the crow, "You have a good voice but don't have common sense."

Moral: Don't trust people who flatter you.

The Dog and His Reflection

A dog was carrying a piece of meat as he walked over a bridge. When he looked down, he saw his reflection in the water. He thought he was seeing another dog holding a piece of meat. The dog quickly opened his jaws to grab what he saw. But in doing this, the meat he had been holding fell from his mouth and sank in the water.

Moral: The person who tries to take what belongs to someone else often loses his own possessions.

The Goose That Laid Golden Eggs

A husband and a wife owned a goose that laid a golden egg every day. Though other people thought they were very lucky, the couple wanted even more gold.

They thought they could find it by cutting open the goose, which they did. But there was no gold in there.

Moral: Be satisfied with what you have.

The Crow and the Pitcher

A thirsty crow came upon a tall pitcher. The pitcher held a little water, but the bird's beak was not long enough to reach it. The crow tried to knock over the pitcher, but it was too heavy. Finally, when almost dead from thirst, the crow saw a pile of pebbles on the ground.

This gave him an idea. The bird dropped the stones, one by one, into the pitcher. This gradually raised the level of the water until finally the crow could drink.

Moral: Sometimes using your brains is a better way of solving a problem than using your muscles.

The Hare and the Hound

A hound came across a hare and began to chase it, thinking the rabbit might make a tasty meal. But after a while, the hare escaped.

A goatherd saw what had happened and made fun of the dog: "The little one runs better than you."

But the hound replied: "I was running only to get something to eat. But the hare was running for his life."

Moral: Our reasons for doing a thing often explain how well we do it.

The Hare and the Tortoise

A speedy hare challenged a slow-moving tortoise to a race. Soon after the start, the hare was so far ahead, he decided he could take a nap and still win. While the hare slept, the tortoise plodded along at a steady pace and eventually passed the snoozing hare. By the time the hare woke, the tortoise neared the finish and won the race.

Moral: Slow and steady wins the race.

The Bear and the Travellers

Two people travelling together were being chased by a hungry-looking bear. When they came to a tree, the first traveller quickly climbed up the trunk without trying to help the other person.

Hoping to avoid being eaten, the traveller on the ground pretended to be dead. The bear sniffed the person's ear. Then, because bears prefer live food, the bear wandered off.

The traveller in the tree climbed down and joked, "What did the bear say to you?"

"He told me not to travel with people who think only of themselves when danger comes."

Moral: When you're in trouble you often find out who your real friends are.

Belling the Cat

The mice were tired of having the cat sneak up on them. One mouse had an idea: "Let's tie a bell around the cat's neck so that we'll be warned if he comes around."

All the other mice thought this was a great idea until a wise old mouse said, "Who among us is going to tie the bell around the cat's neck?"

Moral: Thinking up a plan is easier than carrying it out.

The Boy and the Almonds

A little boy reached into a jar of almonds and filled his hand with as much as it could hold. But then, no matter how hard he tried, he couldn't get the fist full of nuts back out of the jar. Finally, the boy began to cry.

Someone came by and said: "If you drop half the nuts, your fist will be small enough to pull out of the jar.

Moral: Being greedy can get you into trouble.

The Boy Who Cried Wolf

A young shepherd was bored watching the village sheep. One day he decided to have some fun, so he started yelling, "The wolf! The wolf is chasing the sheep!"

People from the village hurried to the field to scare away the wolf. But there was no wolf and the shepherd laughed at them.

A few days later, the shepherd played the same game. This time, the villagers were more angry.

Awhile later, a wolf really came and began to eat the sheep. The boy cried, "Wolf! The wolf is here!" But this time people in the village didn't believe him and no one came to save the sheep.

Moral: If you become known as a liar, people won't believe you even when you tell the truth.

Homonyms

allowed/aloud	its/it's
bare/bear	knight/night
base/bass	knit/nit
beat/beet	knows/nose
boarder/border	lead/led
brake/break	loan/lone
ceiling/sealing	mail/male
cell/sell	main/mane
cent/scent/sent	mall/maul
cereal/serial	miner/minor
chute/shoot	none/nun
coarse/course	oar/ore
council/counsel	pail/pale
days/daze	pain/pane
dear/deer	peace/piece
die/dye	peak/peek
fair/fare	pedal/peddle
feat/feet	plain/plane
flea/flee	plum/plumb
flew/flu/flue	principal/principle
flour/flower	profit/prophet
foul/fowl	read/reed
genes/jeans	read/red
heal/heel/he'll	real/reel
hear/here	right/write
hoarse/horse	ring/wring
hoes/hose	road/rode/rowed
hole/whole	root/route

rote/wrote
sail/sale
scene/seen
shoe/shoo
side/sighed
sole/soul
some/sum
stair/stare
stake/steak
steal/steel
suite/sweet
sundae/Sunday

tail/tale
their/there/they're
threw/through
tide/tied
to/too/two
vain/vane/vein
waist/waste
wait/weight
wear/where
weak/week
weather/whether
whose/who's

Proverbs

A bird in the hand is worth two in the bush.

A chain is only as strong as its weakest link.

A net does not make a fisherman.

A penny saved is a penny earned.

A rolling stone gathers no moss.

A small hole can sink a large ship.

A stitch in time saves nine.

After the ship has sunk, everyone knows how she might have
    been saved.

All sunshine makes a desert.

Birds of a feather flock together.

Don't bite off more than you can chew.

Don't bite the hand that feeds you.

Don't count your chickens before they're hatched.

Don't make a mountain out of a molehill.

Don't put all your eggs into one basket.

Drop by drop fills the tub.

Half a loaf is better than none.

If it isn't broken, don't fix it.

If the shoe fits, wear it.

If you lie down with dogs, you'll get up with fleas.

If you play with fire, you may get burned.

If you want to make an omelet, you have to break some eggs.

Let sleeping dogs lie.

Mighty oaks from little acorns grow.

No use crying over spilled milk.

No use locking the barn door after the horse has been stolen.

One camel does not make fun of the other camel's hump.

One cannot learn to swim in a field.

One man's meat is another man's poison.

One rotten apple spoils the barrel.

People who live in glass houses shouldn't throw stones.

Rome wasn't built in a day.

The early bird catches the worm.

The grass is always greener on the other side of the fence.

The leopard can't change his spots.

The squeaky wheel gets the grease.

Too many cooks spoil the broth.

When in Rome, do as the Romans do.

When the cat's away, the mice will play.

Yesterday's storm causes no damage today.

You can catch more flies with honey than with vinegar.

You can't judge a book by its cover.

You reap what you sow.

Whole Language Reading List

Want to find out more about whole language in general?
Here are some useful books and articles.

The Administrator's Guide to Whole Language by Gail
Heald-Taylor (Richard C. Owen, 1989)

Connections: A Child's Natural Learning Tool by Jane
Baskwill (Scholastic, 1990)

Evaluation: Whole Language, Whole Child by Jane
Baskwill and Paulette Whitman (Scholastic, 1988)

*Finding Our Own Way: Teachers Exploring Their
Assumptions* edited by Judith Newman (Heinemann,
1990)

Grand Conversations: Literature Groups in Action by
Ralph Peterson and Maryann Eeds (Scholastic, 1990)

"Holistic Language Arts" by James Moffett (*Holistic
Education Review*, Spring, 1991, pages 47-55)

Joining the Literacy Club by Frank Smith (Heinemann,
1988)

"Myths of Whole Language" by Judith M. Newman and
Susan M. Church (*The Reading Teacher*, Vol. 44,
No. 1, September 1990, pages 20-26)

Transitions: From Literature to Literacy by Regie
Routman (Heinemann, 1988)

Understanding Whole Language: Principles to Practice by
Constance Weaver (Heinemann, 1990)

What's Whole in Whole Language? by Kenneth Goodman
(Heinemann, 1986)

The Whole Language Catalog edited by Kenneth
Goodman, Lois Bridges Bird, and Yetta Goodman
(American School Publishers, 1991)

Whole Language: Theory in Use edited by Judith
Newman (Heinemann, 1985)

Whole Language: What's the Difference? by Carol
Edelsky, Bess Altwerger, and Barbara Flores
(Heinemann, 1991)

INDEX

Words and phrases that appear in all capital letters are activity names.
The activities are presented in alphabetical order starting on page 7.